In Pursuit of Healthy Love, Vol. 1

*A Guide for the Christian Single...
Seeking Healthy Love in a World of
Deception, Dilemmas, and Lies*

DIANNA SELLS, PH.D.

Professional Christian Counselor

In Pursuit of Healthy Love, Vol. 1
A Guide for the Christian Single . . .
Seeking Healthy Love in a World of Deception, Dilemmas, and Lies
ISBN: 978-1-685730-65-9
Copyright © 2024 by Dianna Sells, Ph.D.

Published by Word and Spirit Publishing
P.O. Box 701403
Tulsa, Oklahoma 74170
wordandspiritpublishing.com

Printed in the United States of America. All rights reserved under International Copyright Law. Content and/or cover may not be reproduced in whole or in part in any form without the expressed written consent of the Publisher.

Dedicated to
all Christian Singles
on their path
to finding healthy love.

CONTENTS

Introduction
vii

Chapter One - Know God's Plan
1

Chapter Two - Date with Intelligence
5

Chapter Three - A Note to the Bereaved and Brokenhearted
15

Chapter Four - Screen Yourself First
17

Chapter Five - Screen with Your Brain
25

Chapter Six - Screen out the Obvious
35

Chapter Seven - Screen with your Gut
41

Chapter Eight - Screen in the Right One for You
49

Screening Tools at a Glance
53

Introduction

It's Complicated—*Dating!*

Dating in this day and age can be scary—and if you're not careful, it can be dangerous. If you are a Christian Single whose heart is to find healthy love, I am writing this book for you. This book should be an easy read that you can slip into your purse. I'll be referring more to women than men, but this book's principles apply to both genders.

- My *hope* is to remove your fears about dating by sparing you from my mistakes.
- My *goal* is to help you find a high-caliber partner with class—who uses kindness and courtesy in thought, word, and deed.
- My *mission* is to use my God-given gifts to help guide you around the pitfalls and traps that I fell into—all dangerous places to find yourself in.
- My *purpose* is to pass on the valuable principles that I learned the hard way in the process of dating

as a divorced Christian Single to those who come behind me.

I am speaking to you heart to heart now, as I will throughout this book. *In Pursuit of Healthy Love, Vol. 1* is a compilation of thirty-plus years of education, expertise, and experience distilled into a short guide to help you as you journey on your venture called dating—or dating again. Know that I found myself many years ago exactly where you find yourself right now. Let us just say, I identify—and I reach out to you today— from my heart to yours.

Chapter 1

Know God's Plan

*"Look, I am sending you out as sheep among wolves.
So be as shrewd as snakes and harmless as doves."*
(Matthew 10:16 NIV)

*"For I know the plans I have for you," declares the Lord,
"plans to prosper you and not to harm you,
plans to give you hope and a future."*
(Jeremiah 29:11 NIV)

Do you find these scriptures in conflict? They are not. God has wonderful plans for you. The warning, however, is that while He is bringing to pass these plans, you must learn to be as shrewd as a snake while being as harmless as a dove.

Merriam Webster states that "shrewd" means to "show sharp powers of judgment; being astute; marked by clever, discerning awareness and acumen; wily and artful in ways of dealing." "Astute" means "an ability to accurately assess situations and people—and turn this to one's advantage." "Acumen" means "keenness and depth of perception, discernment, and discrimination."

Paraphrased, God is saying, "I want you to know that I am, on purpose, sending you out as sheep among wolves—so be sure to show sharp powers of judgment, show yourself to be clever with discerning awareness, keenness, and depth of perception. Use discernment—and discrimination. You need to both have and show an ability to accurately assess situations and people. Be able to turn this assessment to your advantage. Be all this—*but do no harm*."

That's quite a command! How do we fulfill this commandment in Matthew 10:16? Be prepared when the opportunity to date arrives. Do not wing it. "Study to show yourselves approved" (1 Timothy 2:15).

The *New Living Testament* states: "Work hard so you can present yourself to God and receive His approval. Be a good worker, one who does not need to be ashamed and who correctly explains the word of truth."

When dating as a Christian, I had better be prepared; so, I will need the following skills while dating:

- Sharp judgment
- Discernment
- Awareness
- Keenness

- Depth of perception
- Accurate assessment of situations
- Accurate assessment of people
- Turning assessment to advantage
- To do no harm

No small feat, these traits need to be brought into our awareness and developed into a strategy—a plan for dating. God gives us a strategy when He says be "shrewd as snakes," then "harmless as doves."

Chapter 2

Date with Intelligence

You have insight, intelligence, and outstanding wisdom.
(Daniel 5:14)

Connect like a Tortoise: *Cautiously, Wisely, and Slowly*

Now that you know God's plan, know as well that this book is about developing Dating with Intelligence: connecting and establishing a healthy, loving relationship through the process of screening while dating. I will be reminding you often how important it is to *Connect like a Tortoise: Cautiously, Wisely, and Slowly* when dating.

I Moved Way Too Fast

I am authoring this book as a twice-divorced woman who was out there in the trenches for eleven years who moved too fast and made all the mistakes. I had no Dating Intelligence.

I didn't know how to screen. I did not connect cautiously, wisely, or slowly—and I am telling you right now that there is a right way and a wrong way to go about this thing our culture calls "dating."

I have strong, biblically-based moral values, and still did everything wrong. Without boring you with all the details, I violated my cherished values and paid price after price for certain things I did, dating blindly. I learned the hard way that it is just not true that there is no right way or wrong way to date. *There is indeed a right way!*

I Tried All the Wrong Ways

I tried all the wrongs ways, *first*, before I stumbled blindly onto and learned the principles that I am sharing with you in this book. I learned the hard way—and in some cases not the safe way.

"Surely not you!" my friends would say to me. "You've got so much formal education!" You will see, as you read, that Dating Intelligence has nothing to do with formal education.

Before meeting my late husband, Dennis, 21 years ago, I was too vulnerable, too naïve, and too trusting. My timing was too soon after an unwanted divorce. Fortunately, I had begun to learn these principles that I share in this book before Dennis came on the scene 5 years later, and enough time had passed for my own healing after my marriage breakups, or I may have lost Dennis in the process. Thankfully with Dennis, I got it right, or I might have lost him: I believe that.

Formal education has nothing to do with Dating Intelligence. Intellect has nothing to do with Dating Intelligence. I'm smart enough—even educated. These principles that I will share with you have been learned in the School of Hard Knocks. I just happened to be educated as a Professional Christian Counselor while going through the process. Looking back, I'm sure that God was teaching me everything I did wrong, so I could author this book to pass on to you one day. In that, I have no doubt.

But What About Dating in This Current Age?

You may ask, "Aren't the rules for today different?" All you have to do is visit an online dating website to see for yourself. The need for "Dating Intelligence," such as this book offers, smacks me right between the eyes as huge. Up to this point in time, however, the need has yet to be met—through the book market, anyway. This book fulfills that need.

In the midst of dating, I got it all backward. I walked a precarious path I'd never wish on any person due to my own, shall I say, ignorance? Perhaps a better term might be a simple lack of knowledge as to what I was doing—a lack of Dating Intelligence.

As far as using any wisdom, you can forget it. In the beginning, I simply lacked Dating Intelligence. Just suffice it to say, think the worst about possible outcomes when it comes to dating. I more than likely lived it.

My Story, Briefly

This book is not an autobiography, but I'll give you a few tidbits about my life. After my unwanted breakup after 21 years of my first marriage, I made a mess of things. I met over coffee or dinner the dredges who were online. I dated too soon, too broken, too vulnerable, and too naïve. I slept around, violated my cherished Christian values, had two attempted date rapes, and within three years of my 21-year marital breakup, I had quickly connected to and married a highly polished and smooth con artist who took me over the next seven years for $1.1M, and left me high and dry to the tune of $67K in debt for a woman worth $10-20M. This is just the bare bones—the highlights of my rocky road to finding real and healthy love.

How Could I Have Allowed It?

You may wonder how I could have allowed it, because I honestly should have known better. Looking back, however, I think I was at least a little bit desperate—*okay, a lot desperate*—to find love. I didn't even fathom the concept of healthy love back then. I wasn't like the tortoise: I didn't connect cautiously. I didn't connect wisely. I didn't connect slowly. I did all the wrong things, amid wrong timing, for all the wrong reasons, *and opened myself up to deception.*

The interesting thing about deception is that once you are in deception, you don't know you are being deceived. You don't walk around saying, "Hey! I'm in deception!" You don't even know you're in it. You just are—*being deceived.* Until it's too late, when you wake up to the reality of what has happened to you and all the damage that's been done. Through this process, I learned that *when you need to be loved more than you need to know truth, you open yourself to deception.*

Open your eyes (to see!). Trust your gut (to sense!). I made the mistakes I made because I *blinded* myself to truths about the men that I was dating that I didn't *want* to see or *know* when dating. Don't be like me! Go in with your eyes wide open, trusting your gut (*with impressions from the Holy Spirit*) to speak to you.

The Tough Question

Why is it that many, if not most, dating Christian Singles embrace the scriptures, except for the passages about sex? As a dating Christian Single out in the world of deception and lies, you need to decide what you stand for. Do you embrace all the scriptures, or just some of them, leaving out the parts about sex? Why? One primary reason is because having sex before marriage is expected in this current age. Another reason is that sex meets a "feel-good" need you have, and fuels dreams you have—dreams that may never come to pass with sex in the equation.

The Purpose of Dating

"Aren't finding love and hopefully marriage the primary purposes of dating?" you may ask. This may shock you, but the primary purpose of healthy dating is to know and strengthen yourself first, because healthy dating is at first a spiritual and conceptual process—not an emotional one, *and certainly not a sexual one.*

Starting out, during the first stages of dating, dating is not emotional, though our society would make you think it's all about the feel-good emotions. I imagine that this is going to be one of your foremost challenges when applying the principles you learn in this book: to accept the fact that healthy dating is a slow, slow, slow process—like the crockpot or the tortoise; not a fast, or an emotional—or even sexual—process. Finding healthy love is one by-product of a healthy dating relationship, and putting sex on the front burner of that special dating process won't make that happen. *To make that happen you must go in with Dating Intelligence.*

Develop Dating Intelligence

Dating Intelligence is an investigative process – analytical, with fact-gathering – while building mutual respect. Once you have thoroughly screened the man (or woman) you have an eye for, there will be plenty of time for emotion later.

May the Forces Be with You

I'm taking you into the complex shadow world of hidden dynamics, mysteries, and forces working for you or against you as you are dating—for good or for ill—and teaching you how to recognize them. By the time you are putting these principles of Dating Intelligence into practice, you will have earned your master's degree in dating.

My Motivation in Writing

Do I want to sell a million books? Do *I want In Pursuit of Healthy Love, Vol. 1* to be a bestseller? My answer is this: will it get the word out that these principles exist? Will it help millions of single men and women who need these principles? Will it change lives? Will it help men and women find healthy love? Then, yes, I pray it's a bestseller and sells millions of books.

Know my heart, however, that my motivation is not money—it's for enlightenment of dating Christian Singles, it's changing lives, and hopefully of persuading just one single—maybe you—to try the practical principles I offer, so you can see, firsthand, the value of the principles I am sharing in your own life and future relationship.

Keep Reading

In this book, I'm going to share things that will bristle you—maybe I already have! I may say things that make the hair stand up on the back of your neck, perhaps even make you mad and want to throw the book down. Be prepared for that—then keep reading. Especially if you find yourself up against the same patterns of failure in your dating process that you've had many times before, I urge you to learn that there's *a unique and better way to go about dating*.

This unique process may feel counterintuitive at first because it goes against current thinking about what is expected on a date and the "anything goes" mentality of our day. This unique way to go about dating is by using Dating

Intelligence and learning how to Screen, Screen, Screen—screen out and screen in.

Why do Principles of Dating Intelligence Work?

You are on a learning curve. Give yourself a chance to try this book's principles before you get out the matches and try to burn it. The principles work. No, these principles are not a game. They are not the effortless way to do it: they are more difficult, you'll find—but Dating Intelligence is the way that works.

With Dating Intelligence, you are putting into practice Universal Principles—principles based in Scripture, setting them free to work on your behalf for you, rather than your giving into the forces that will work against you—forces that violate your values.

I ask that you read front to back, I hope in one sitting; then after that, use this book as a reference guide for screening out the potential dating partners not meant for you personally. Then find and screen in the right person for you in every way. Ladies, a more modern way to say this is that by applying these principles you are screening out the bad boys, and screening in the good guys. Gentlemen, you're screening out the bad girls, and screening in the good ones.

So, Which Are You?

If you are that single who would just rather continue doing what he or she has been doing when dating, getting the same results, who does not care to learn new ways to go about a process as ancient as the Bible itself, then knock yourself out—*but read this book anyway.* You may learn something you did not know before, even one small point that can change the direction of dating for you and your life.

Perhaps you are a man or woman *In Pursuit of Healthy Love* who wants to meet a high-caliber partner and break the patterns you are currently experiencing in your dating life. This book is for you.

Maybe you are just starting out dating for the first time.

Maybe you are already dating right now.

Perhaps you are divorced or widowed and starting over.

Perhaps you are thinking about the idea of dating, but for whatever reason you are fearful of trying.

For all of you, men and women alike, these principles of Dating Intelligence are for you, for your protection. With this guide in your hand, you don't have to make the mistakes I did. Rest assured, amid your fears about dating, there's hope for you through *In Pursuit of Healthy Love, Vol. 1*, as I guide you through the process of connecting like a tortoise: cautiously, wisely, and slowly—by learning how to screen up front the person you are dating, to **screen out** or to **screen in**.

Chapter 3

A Note to the Bereaved and Brokenhearted

*The Lord is near to the brokenhearted
and saves the crushed in spirit.*
(Psalm 34:18)

I'll jump right in and give you a rule of thumb: if you currently are grieving with a broken heart over the loss of a love, you need to take the number of months or years you had been together, divide that number by 5, and know that this is the minimum number of months or years it will take you to grieve and feel "normal" again. Until then, you are putting the pieces of your life back together; you are healing and most vulnerable.

Remember once you are broken-hearted, and grieving, you stand to be extremely vulnerable to all the wrong things, you stand to much more easily make the wrong choices. You may, for instance, fall too easily into the hands of a charmer who preys on you for your money, or fall too easily for sexual seduction, way too soon. (I did.)

Not a fun thought. Grief is not a fun process to have to navigate, but its voice speaks loudly—you have been affected and you cannot push the process ahead of its time. So, go ahead and read this book, and keep it for the right time, for when you are healed and ready to begin dating again.

Wait, however, for that time—and in the meantime seek healing through prayer, singles' groups, meditation, and counseling. Hope is on the other side of grief, but dating during grief can spell future trouble for any relationship you may find along the way. You are not going to want to do this, but you need to heal before you start to date.

Now, let's get started teaching you how to screen for healthy love by applying the principles of Dating Intelligence in this book—starting with being self-responsible. I'll see you in Chapter 4.

Chapter 4

Screen Yourself First

Choose for yourself this day whom you will serve.
(Joshua 24:15)

Safety First

Dating is not a game. It's not just something you jump into one day—it is your life on the line. Your number one responsibility when dating should always be safety. Safety first!

Read that again.

I'm not talking about only physical safety, but spiritual safety and emotional safety. Safety during years to come, safety for your children, for your home, for your finances—they all fall under Safety First.

You may be thinking as many do, "I can protect myself." I was one of those women at one time. I'm sure you can protect yourself. Shoot! You may even have a black belt in karate. The principles I am sharing with you, however, fall into a whole other category than physical strength.

To Implement Safety First, Begin to Build Your *Screening Toolbox*

To protect yourself spiritually, physically, emotionally, and mentally, let's begin with some self-reflection. I am presuming you are single, or single again. You want to think about dating again, or you have already started dating and are not happy with the results you are getting.

It's Time to Discover the WHO within YOU

Ask yourself these tough questions—and take just moment to answer them.

1. *Who am I when I'm single and alone compared with when I am in a relationship with another?* Does that change? Am I the same person when dating and in relationship as I am right now when I'm single and alone? If not, what changes?
2. *What do I believe about myself?* Am I worthy of finding real and healthy love? What do I base this belief upon? Can another person love me for who I am just the way I am? What positives pop up into my mind when I ask myself these questions?
3. *What are my values?* My value system is what I value in my life—it's the compilation of my core values that

make up who I am. What do I value most in my life that I *refuse* to compromise while I am dating?

4. *What is my purpose in dating?* Am I looking for companionship, friendship, or marriage? Or am I out just to have a good time?

5. *What do I believe about sex before marriage?* Settle yourself on this awkward issue right now because you can rest assured it will pop its head up early on when texting, talking by phone, or going out in our culture. Know what you believe on this issue, make it a values issue, and use it as a screening tool when getting to know one another. Biblically, GOD says to wait until marriage.

Add your own questions to the list and pray quietly and deeply about how you view yourself and what parts about yourself are *not* to be changed or compromised for another person.

If you don't respect yourself, no one else will.

You must know who you are and what you want in a dating relationship before you ever respond to that first text, answer that first phone call, or step out your front door to go for that first coffee.

Dating starts with prayer, knowing how you view yourself, and developing respect for that self that GOD created. Don't just wing it! If you don't know who you are, how can you share who that person is with another person in the initial stages of dating?

The worst thing you can do is to pretend with a man or woman in the first stages of dating on topics such as sex before marriage, then go back on your word later. You may say you want to wait, but after a period of time, you give in and have sex before marriage. The person you are with will wonder what else you have lied about or pretended about. To build respect with the person you are dating, be firm in your convictions. Take a stand, then don't change it.

> *Therefore, take up the full armor of God, so that when the day of evil comes, you will be able to stand your ground, and having done all, then stand.* (Ephesians 6:13)

Be Clear with Yourself Before Ever Going on A Date

If you're having a tough time answering self-reflection questions, that's normal at first. It's vital you think about them, however. Begin now to get clear with yourself:

- *Know what you believe about yourself and hold to it.*
- *Know your values and assert them.*
- *Know your purpose for dating and let it guide you.*

As you date, these insights will guide you in the process to know if someone, right up front, is a possibility for long-term dating or not. If not, you can move on more quickly and not waste your precious time with someone who was a dead end from the beginning. While self-reflecting, write down the answers to these few critical questions:

- What things do I *refuse* to live *without*?
- What things do I *refuse* to live *with*?
- What things are *negotiable* for me?
- What things are *non-negotiable* for me?

Before you ever walk out that door on a first date, you should have the answers to these simple questions in your Screening Toolbox to pull out and look at privately when a topic of discussion comes up, or a question that requires an answer. Above all be honest with yourself and with the person you are on the date with. Never pretend you are someone or something you are not.

Your Most Important Screening Tool

*Your **value system** is the most powerful screening tool you have in your possession to either attract a good dating partner or to repel an unworthy one.*

Answer what do you **value** in your life that you *refuse* to live without? What do you *refuse* to live with? Then stand your ground. If someone refuses to date you because of your values, or even a single value that you have, move on—let that person go. Nothing—no, nothing—is worth the violation of your value system.

Become What You Want to Attract

When I say become what you want to attract, I'm not saying change the who within you. I'm saying if you want to attract a polished man or classy woman, begin now fixing up before you go out. Dress like yourself, but in clothes that will attract the kind of person you like. Personally, I like earthy men, so I loved to dress in jeans and boots and go out in something earthy looking. It's just my style.

What is your style? Dress now with the idea in mind that the man or woman you hope to find is sitting in the next booth to you having coffee, or in that line at the grocery store, or in the bookstore browsing books. You just never know. Don't forget that the right man or woman is looking for you too, so fix up a bit before you go out.

It wouldn't hurt to start taking some selfies of yourself now and then too when you look especially good that day. Or even better have a friend you may be out with take a picture of you when you are out shopping or on a run or biking or having lunch. You'll need these showing the many aspects of your personality if you ever decide to put yourself out there on an online dating website—the full spectrum of you, showing your interests. Perhaps take photos of yourself with your dog or with your kids. Natural, fun, engaging. Do you like to golf? Show a photo of yourself club in hand on the course. Do you like to bike? Show yourself standing next to your bike with helmet and glasses. Above all, avoid the cleavage, tacky, nude, and cheesy shots if you want to attract a high-caliber, mature man or woman.

Remember, become what you want to attract. Women who put up sensual and sexual photos online are just asking for the guys looking for sex to come calling. I mean do you really walk around all day pursing your lips like a fish? Men, the fastest way to turn off a first-class lady is to put up sexual photos of yourself!

Take photos of yourself that are natural, on the go, and fun if you want to attract a quality guy or gal. Closeups and long-distance photos are good as well. Become comfortable in front of the camera in your body. If you don't like your body right now, go on a health plan to drop a few pounds, then begin taking photos and start dating. I'll tell you now, however, that not all men are looking for skinny women—many men like women who are a little overweight. I had a man tell me once when I was dating online that he loved "fluffy" women. Some short men love tall women. Try to realize and believe right now, if you can, that the right guy or gal is out there for you—he or she just needs to find you. Your job is to make that happen—*connecting cautiously, wisely, and slowly, Dating Intelligently!* Learn how to screen with your brain, as you'll find in Chapter 5. See you there.

Chapter 5

Screen with Your Brain

*"Do not conform to the patterns of this world,
but be transformed by the renewing of your mind.
Then you will be able to test and approve what God's will is...."*
(Romans 12:2)

NEXT!

To date in this culture, you've got to get tough. You've got to do two things: you must start thinking of your early dating *objectively*, as a form of "field research," using your brain, and you must learn how to use the door-slam term "NEXT!" Then move on.

A Side Note

When doing field research, the door slam is a figure of speech. It's not literal. It's something you choose to do in your mind, saying "NEXT," slamming the door emotionally to that person as a possibility, for whatever reason you feel they are not for you, and move on.

The way you move on is to be kind and respectful to the man or woman you are slamming the door on, but the door to that possibility in your mind has been shut, bolted, and irrevocably closed. There is no need to address with the person the reason—it's just not working for you. All you need to do is say simply, "This is just not working for me. I'm sorry." Matter of fact and kind. Then move on.

Dating Intelligently

Your mindset in the first stages of dating is critical. Your mindset must be one of *integrity, objectivity, common sense, and sanity.*

- With *integrity*, you set your mind not to compromise your core beliefs, values, or purpose in dating—no matter what! No matter how hot he is, sexy he is, perfect in every other way he is, if you are a Christian and value that in a guy, but he's not, then he's not the one God has for you in the long term. If you don't want a guy who smokes, and he smokes, he's not the one. Say NEXT. Then move on.

- With *objectivity*, you set your mind to use your brain and guard your heart while dating. Period.

    Above all else, guard your heart, for everything you do flows from it. . . . Give careful thought to the paths for your feet and be steadfast in all your ways. (Proverbs 4:23-27)

When a guy you are attracted to isn't attracted back, you move on. You don't get your feelings hurt—ever! Ladies, don't chase—ever! Don't pursue—ever! Say NEXT in your heart. Then move on. Remember that biblically the man does the pursuing. This is for your protection.

- With **common sense**, you set your mind to use sound judgment when going out to meet someone early on. *Remember safety first!* You don't put yourself in compromising situations, alone in his apartment or in his car or on a dark street together early on. You don't know this guy yet. You don't even know if he's safe, yet. If he pushes you to violate your sound judgment, say NEXT. Then move on. (By the way, I blew it with this one repeatedly, embarrassing to say, and ended up with two attempted date rapes. Don't be like me. It matters.)

- With **sanity**, you set your mind to keep your emotions and your wits about you. One of the cornerstones of mental health is dedication to reality. *Your job is to stay grounded in reality — not fantasy!*

This will be a hard one, because when you are caught up in the throes of cathexis (infatuation), fantasy tries to reign. You must keep your feet solidly on the ground, remember your commitment to your values, and purpose at these moments to keep your wits about you—especially during this early stage of dating.

The Importance of Projecting Self-Respect

The number two goal, after the number one goal of safety first, is to build a dating partner's respect for you. Real love grows out of the soil of respect: it doesn't grow out of desire, nor emotion, nor sex. Remember this, ladies: *Sex will never get a man. Sex will never keep a man.*

Sex early on just clouds the equation, creates an imbalance in the relationship. The woman becomes more needy of the man while the man becomes more bored early on.

Mutual respect—which is your goal—starts with your having *self-respect*. How can he respect you if you behave in a way that doesn't show respect for yourself? From the moment you meet, you are training a man what to think about you. Not "feel" for, but "think" about you.

Do you present yourself as sexy, or demure? That is part of your résumé that he is logging into his head. What values do you have that you present right up front to a man by how you dress, how you talk, how you conduct yourself? If you want to attract class in a man, you must become class—you must operate with kindness and courtesy in thought, word, and deed. Keep sexuality on the back burner.

It's part of who you are, but it's not who you want to present right off the bat to a man. Always remember to respect yourself in your words, attitudes, and behaviors, and he will respect you as well. For example, ladies, dress to direct his eyes to your face, not your body. If you are going to show skin, show one area: a shoulder perhaps, your ankles, or a calf, your neck, certainly not cleavage, back, shoulders, and thighs all at once. Get the picture?

Both men and women, present yourself with self-respect from the beginning keeping your values straight, and she/he will respect you for it, and you will more than likely keep his/her interest. Ladies, if all a man wants is sex, and you want to wait, he may quickly move on—this is a good thing!

Powerful Screening Tools

Your values and self-respect are two of the most powerful screening tools you have in your Screening Toolbox to either attract the right man or repel the wrong man. Learning how to do both is equally important. You don't want to waste your time on the wrong man for you. The right one is still trying to find you.

How Does Love Grow?

Love grows one way: from the soil of respect. If you both find you have self-respect and respect for one another, then love has a chance to grow in the future. He'll never forget your first impression that you made with him. You'll never forget his first impression, either. Establish self-respect in how you dress, what you say, how you think, and how you behave.

No, Dating Is Not about This

Dating is not about "hunka hunka burning love," as Elvis used to belt out on his guitar. Our society, however, would make you think that's what it's for: to find your "hunka hunka burning love."

Laying the foundation for love to grow is about one thing: building mutual respect.

Ask yourself, on this date, what am I saying, thinking, and doing that show that I respect myself? Is he doing the same? Are we learning to enjoy and respect each other at the same time while not creating a threat to the growth of the dating relationship?

Observe Each Other through the Four Seasons

If you have as one of your purposes to be married one day to the man or woman of your dreams, be prepared to date at the very least through the four seasons—face to face, not long distance. Better yet, do that twice.

Why are the four seasons critical? You learn a great deal that you didn't know about a person during the holidays, summer months, winter months, spring, and autumn. Food likes and dislikes appear, seasonal sports interests crop up, beliefs rise to the surface.

I was getting to know a man I had met online as we were approaching the Christmas holiday season. We had not met in person yet, and were talking by phone, when I mentioned how much my children love to decorate the tree. He jumped in and said, "Oh, I don't allow a tree. We believe in Winter Solstice only."

This was a clear NEXT.

Another time, I had been dating a man for a few months as Valentine's Day was approaching. On the day, I gave him a small, appropriate gift, which he took in hand and put down on the table, saying, "I don't believe in Valentine's Day, and I don't believe in Valentine's Day gifts." He gave my gift back to me.

NEXT.

Another time (I have many examples!), I had been talking long distance with a man for a few months who flew into town so we could meet over a weekend. It happened to fall on his birthday, so I bought him an inexpensive, but nice James Avery Christian man's pinky ring. Upon opening it, he said, "Oh, I don't wear silver—only gold." He put the ring back in the box without ever trying it on and proceeded to hand it back to me.

NEXT.

Another time, one sweltering summer, I had been talking, again, long distance, to a man from California when I lived in Oklahoma at the time. He was driving through the state on his way somewhere and wanted to meet and take me to dinner. First, he showed up at my door in short, cropped jeans, a ½ inch below his bottom in length, with no shirt on and wearing boots. I was shocked. I said, "I'm not going anywhere with you looking like that." (Screen #1 fail). Once he changed his clothes, we went somewhere casual, and when he sat across from me, while he was talking, his eyes would bulge out, and his tongue would shoot straight out, over again in a highly animated fashion. This went on the entire time he was talking. (Screen #2 fail.) Then to top the evening off, when the food came, he became stone-cold silent. Not a word through his entire meal. When I asked him why he stopped talking, he said curtly, "I'm eating." Then went back to his meal. (Screen #3 fail.)

NEXT.

Winter months, springtime, summer, and autumn, Valentine's Day, Memorial Day weekend, Independence Day, Labor Day Weekend, Halloween, Thanksgiving, Christmas, and New Year's Eve and Day—as well as birthdays, your children's birthdays, daily outings, dinners out, weekends away, vacations—all will speak volumes to you about the patterns and beliefs of the man or woman you are dating.

Be the tortoise: allow time to pass so you can see exactly what you are getting yourself into in a variety of settings if the dating relationship is to become long-term.

Ladies, Give Him the Gift of the Chase

- A man loves to pursue! Please do not take that joy away from him by pursuing. *Your job in the beginning is to attract*, not pursue. Attract, not pursue. Let him pursue, not you. Put yourself out there so the right man can find you, *then wait*. The right man will come along one day, not unlike the proverbial needle in the haystack. In the meantime, be prepared to run into a lot of hayseeds. It's part of the dating process, especially if you have opted to turn to online dating.

- Every man loves the chase! It's how he's wired. To rob him of the chase is like robbing him of part of the fun of the dating process. This means holding off on jumping to the finish line with sex right out of the chute.

I cannot emphasize enough how important it is to keep sex on the back burner while going through the screening process early on in dating. The Bible, as you know, says to wait until marriage. I am not here to preach to you, but if you can wait, there is a reason God tells us this: the man needs the chase! The longer you hold off on sex, the more the chase within him will build and the more his desire will grow and the more time you will be giving his emotions to catch up with this desire.

In the meantime, your job is to develop the 4 P's:

- Patience - resilience and fortitude to keep you steady.

- Perseverance - tenacity and grit to give you strength.

- Polish - class and style to attract a high caliber man.

- Poise - calm and composure to keep you at rest internally while you wait.

How's your Screening Toolbox so far? It should be filling up with wonderful tools to screen out and screen in with. So, let's move on to screening for the stuff you can see—the obvious. See you in Chapter 5.

P.S. . . . bring your Screening Toolbox, so far, with you.

Your Screening Tools So Far

1. Safety first.
2. Self-respect second.
3. Connect like a tortoise: *cautiously, wisely, slowly.*
4. Know the things I value in my life.
5. Know my purpose in dating.
6. Know who I am at my core.
7. Know what I believe about myself.
8. Know what things I *refuse* to live *without.*
9. Know what things I *refuse* to live *with.*
10. Know what things I find *negotiable.*
11. Know what things I find *non-negotiable.*
12. Operate with integrity—being true to myself.
13. Operate with objectivity—seeing things with detachment.
14. Operate with common sense—using sound judgment.
15. Operate with sanity—keeping my emotions and wits about me.
16. Becoming what I want to attract.
17. Using patience.
18. Exercising perseverance.
19. Presenting polish.
20. Reflecting poise.
21. Ladies, give him the gift of the chase.

22. Men, pursue.
23. Go through the 4 seasons.
24. Keep sex on the back burner.
25. Sex will never get a man, sex will never keep a man.
26. Add to this list the things you want to remember.

Chapter 6

Screen Out the Obvious

"By their fruit you will recognize them. Do people pick grapes from thorn bushes, or figs from thistles?"
(Matthew 7:16)

This Chapter is to use your Screening Toolbox to screen concretely—for the stuff that is readily apparent.

Read His Résumé

His résumé is not written on paper. It's how he presents himself to you right out of the chute, how well he treats you, how he treats other people, how he behaves, and things he says and tells you about himself.

Remember, it's a résumé—sometimes people lie about themselves on their résumé. So be aware that could happen. You need to observe—*over time*—to see if what he is telling you about himself, his family, his friends, his dreams, and his work history are all true.

He is both *telling* you and *showing* you who he really is. Listen carefully, because odds are that an honest man will tell you a lot about himself, and once he does, listen, because you need to believe what he says about what he wants in a relationship.

- If he says he doesn't want to marry, but only wants to find a friend who wants to be "friends with benefits," he means it.
- If he says he's only looking for companionship, he means it.
- If he says he's still married but in the middle of a divorce, then you will want to rethink seeing this man—not a good timing for either of you.
- If he is just looking to "hook up," (have sex!) he means it.
- If he tells you he never plans to marry again, believe it.

If any of these things don't ring true with your values, say NEXT, and move on.

Is there Physical Attraction?

No, this isn't all there is to a relationship, but it is a critical part. Chemistry plays a huge role in an intimate relationship over time, though it needs to not be front and center in the first stages of screening. It's good to know it's there. Be aware of the chemistry, or lack thereof.

Does He Have A Short Fuse or A Temper?

These are the days in dating when most people put their best foot forward. You may not see this if it does exist until much later in the dating scene. You may, however, see it early on. It may take the form of impatience with a waiter or a bellhop, or a snappy retort to you.

A quick temper is not a good sign for problem solving and communication. It could be a symptom of a much bigger problem or disorder, so keep an eye out for this. A quick temper is an impulse control issue and not to be ignored. Be forewarned.

Does He Use Foul Language?

Does it violate your values? Then tell him you'd prefer he doesn't use such language in your presence. If you get resistance, or it continues, say NEXT. Move on.

Is He Too Charming?

I used to tell my daughter when she was growing up and began dating, "Beware the man with chiseled cheeks." When someone is too packaged, too put together, too charming, too over-the-top, flashes too much money, trying too hard to impress, just too much overall, beware. Beware the TOO as a signal something may be off.

Charming is okay, as it may come with the territory with some men, but TOO charming, watch out for. Are you familiar with the term "love bombing?" If he's overdoing it with the flowers, gifts, flowery language, and love language too soon—TOO charming—watch out.

Narcissists love to "love bomb" you early on—starting with the inappropriate and extravagant gifts way too soon, giving the impressions that he's the "ideal" love for you. Demanding commitment from you way too soon, or demanding anything at all, feeling "entitled" to you (your time, your attention), resisting the boundaries you set, saying "I love you" right out of the chute, making immediate promises with you they can't or won't keep—just overall trying to impress you way too much, way too soon—beware. These are all huge signals that you need to keep on your toes with this one and guard your heart. Maybe even say NEXT and move on.

What Does He Bring to the Table as Relational Baggage?

You need to keep an ear out for how many times he has been divorced, or if he has never been married before. Does he have children? How many? What is his relationship with his ex like? Are they on friendly terms, or does he tear her down? If so—not a good sign.

You may be 50 and decide you don't want to date a fifty-year-old bachelor—because all his energies and money have been spent on himself his whole life. Something to consider. Keep an eye out for whether he is more selfish or reluctant to marry than a man who has been married with children, who has had to share and give of himself more through his relationship history. Also consider that a life-long bachelor may not understand the dynamics of a true, intimate partnership, and the older he is, the more difficult these dynamics may be to learn. These are just things to consider when looking at relational baggage.

You may be able to add to this list of things that are readily apparent, but as you can see, the list isn't long. You might ask yourself these questions as well when screening what is readily apparent:

- Does he cook? Love to cook? Hate to cook? Does he dine out most of the time? What does this say about how he spends his money?
- Does he tend to dress up? Dress down? Do you like what you see?
- Does he drink? Not drink? What do you prefer?
- Does he talk too much? Not enough? Just right? Who does he talk about? Himself? Does he ask you questions about yourself?

- What subjects does he enjoy talking about? Spiritual things? Cars and motorcycles? Rodeos? Do you find his objects for discussion interesting?

- What is his social intelligence? How does he treat others he meets?

What do the answers to these questions tell you about your date? Is he someone you are attracted to? Or not?

You will find screening out the readily apparent things is the easy part. The more difficult things to screen out are where you must screen intuitively, trusting your gut to guide you, addressed in Chapter 7.

Chapter 7

Screen with Your Gut

And the peace of God, which transcends all understanding will guard your hearts and your minds in Christ Jesus.
(Philippians 4:7)

Always Move in the Way of Peace

Using our Dating Intelligence learned so far, now we move from the seen to the unseen. *How do we see the unseen? With our gut.* Our internal radar, our intuition, speaks within us. We just need to listen with open ears and not ignore the red flags our gut shows us. Our gut, with the impression given to us by the Holy Spirit, will confirm the good stuff with peace—and reject the potentially damaging or imbalanced stuff we are experiencing with another person. We must listen to it.

- Some hidden, even mysterious, dynamics that you will experience with another person that will either set well with your gut, or not, include some of the following forces:

- family forces;
- communication style and flow;
- independence versus dependence;
- fire and ice;
- energy balance or imbalance;
- spacing and pacing;
- red flags;
- misalignment of interests;
- emotional age;
- mental disorders;
- and others.

When negative forces are at work that you are feeling in your gut, you will feel a tug, or lack of peace, or intuitive disturbance in your gut that needs to be addressed within yourself, and perhaps with your dating partner. Let's briefly address a few of these below.

Family Forces

We are raised in homes that bring forces into our lives that we are subject to until at least age 16. That's why it's important, if you can, to investigate a person's family background. The family extremes we may have been affected by include rigid to chaotic, disengaged to enmeshed—some blend of these. The healthiest family system is none of these extremes but is called "flexibly connected."

We bring these same forces with us into a home and family system we try to set up with a partner. As you could imagine, if you came out of a highly ordered, rigid family system with rigid rules and roles and you pick a partner who was raised in a chaotic family system where anything goes, there could be a problem merging the two systems when setting up a living arrangement with a dating partner.

You may have come from an enmeshed family system, where everyone tends to think alike and know each other's business but pick a partner from a disengaged system where little connection takes place between family members and little is known about others within the family. This again could cause problems.

Take time to get to know the type of family system you both come out of. This does not mean you cannot make a partnership work, but if you can compromise and strive to develop a "flexibly structured" system that is not too extreme in the areas of rigidity versus chaotic, or enmeshed versus disengaged, you can make great strides in making a relationship work for you. Allow your gut to guide you.

Communication Style and Flow

I dated a man once that stole the conversation from the get-go and never let it go. His view of conversation was a monologue, not a dialogue. Mine was to dialogue. I became horribly bored as he never paused so I could join the conversation and talked so fast that I couldn't understand him. To say the least this dating relationship did not last. Mutual communication interests and energy and speed can make a stark difference in whether you are comfortable day to day just simply trying to communicate with your partner.

If the person you are dating wants to communicate on a concrete level about what happened today, what he did, who he saw, etc. and you enjoy communicating on an introspective level about how you have been feeling today, what has happened within you, wanting to communicate on the same level with a partner, you may have some compromising to do. Which are you? Odds are your partner is the opposite. Allow your gut to guide you.

Independence vs. Dependence

If you are one to stand on your own two feet and your partner wants to lean on you emotionally, you may be more independent of a partner and your partner may be more dependent on you. This is also known in our culture as "codependency." Since opposites do seem to attract, this is not an unusual pairing but one that may need some tweaking so that the independent individual doesn't feel resentful of the dependent partner for leaning too hard. Which are you? Odds are your partner is the opposite. Allow your gut to guide you.

Fire and Ice

People tend to be temperamentally either warm or cool toward others. In an unhealthy relationship, they may pair up hot and cold! In a partnership, many couples find themselves pairing up warm with cool. It shouldn't be a problem. A more compatible pairing would be warm with warm or cool with cool. Which are you? Odds are your partner is the opposite. Allow your gut to guide you.

Energy Balance vs. Imbalance

Bringing *mutual* emotional energy into a relationship is vital to a healthy partnership—to developing healthy love. When one partner carries the greater portion of the emotional energy, typically the warmer partner, and the cooler partner carries less of the emotional energy, the odds are that the warmer partner will feel less loved and more in pursuit of that love from the cooler partner, while the cooler partner will feel more annoyed and put upon in the relationship—more bored. The ideal is when a *mutual* energy flows back and forth between both people.

Ladies, if you find yourself as the warmer dating partner, be careful not to pursue the man, but think of yourself as on a teeter-totter—when the cooler partner pulls back, instead of stepping forward, step back a bit. Allow the cooler one room to move forward toward you. Allow your gut to guide you.

Pacing and Spacing

When dating, how fast you wish to move in the relationship (pacing) and how often you wish to see one another (spacing) more than likely varies from partner to partner. These are two dynamics that need to be *verbally* discussed over time for clarity between you.

- You want to see him daily, yet he wants to see you weekly is a spacing issue.
- He wants to have sex on the first date, yet you want to wait until you are married is a pacing issue.

Clarify these issues as they arise. Don't bury them under the rug, or resentments and problems will fester from the beginning of your dating. Allow your gut to guide you.

Red Flags

A strong, negative, or fearful gut reaction to something a dating partner says or does more than likely is a "red flag." A red flag is an intuitive warning signal: don't go there, don't date this person, or date this person cautiously until you know if your gut is right. Allow your gut to guide you as to whether this is a positive or negative pairing. Does he drink too much? Does he continually use foul language? Does he always bring the subject back around to sex?

Remember Safety First! Avoid red flags at all costs. You may not know why, but your gut is giving you a warning signal you must listen to if you are to stay out of danger. In my second marriage, I was so desperate to find love that when I heard red flags coming from him that deeply bothered me, I ignored them. That marriage ultimately became a disaster when later I discovered that he was a con artist.

GOD will send red flags to protect you while you are dating. Mind the red flags! Don't ignore them. Ignore them at your own peril.

Misalignment of Interests

If your many interests align, yay for you! However, when you find yourself bored with what interests your date, you know within yourself this more than likely isn't going to go anywhere. NEXT. Allow your gut to guide you.

Emotional Age

In unhealthy dating relationships, one of the problems may be that your dating partner may act like a 15-year-old—all the while he is 45 years old biological age. This person will be acting "childish," as opposed to "childlike."

Being childlike, with favorable qualities, such as having fun, is not the same as being childish, with unfavorable qualities—being immature or juvenile.

If you discover he is immature and continues to act juvenile, you may decide it's time to say NEXT. If you don't, ladies, you'll be dating and perhaps one day marrying someone who becomes like your teenage son. Men, you'll feel like you're a father rather than a husband. Allow your gut to guide you.

Mental Disorders

If you have an inkling in your gut that you may be dealing with a mental disorder in your date, it's time to do a little concrete research. For looking into mental disorders while dating, refer to the Diagnostic Statistical Manual of Mental Disorders (DSM-5). Many of the red flags you feel in your gut toward someone are symptomatic of their having mental disorders, from bipolar 1 to narcissistic personality disorder to borderline personality disorder, to oppositional defiant disorder, a/k/a passive aggressive disorder, to dependency disorder, a/k/a codependency, to scores of others. This manual would be a suitable place to start to do more research on what you are seeing or hearing that is stirring in your gut like a red flag. To start, go to the section on "Personality Disorders."

If you're feeling guilty, don't. You'd test drive a vehicle doing your research longer than you would be researching the person you are dating. Get the facts, then get in touch with your gut—your intuition! Trust it. If it begins to stir inside you, give heed to it. Your gut is a reaction to an instinctive emotional response rather than considered thought. Trust your gut every time. It's called "trusting your gut instinct." Listen to your gut, listen to your intuition. Say NEXT. Allow your gut to guide you.

Chapter 8

Screen In the Right One for You

Let us not become weary in doing good, for at the proper time we will reap a harvest if we do not give up.
(Galatians 6:9)

So far, as we've been building your Screening Toolbox and educating you on developing Dating Intelligence, we've done a lot of Screening *Out* by saying NEXT and moving on. Now let's look at traits we want in a person that we date and want to Screen *In*, taken from Galatians 5.

The following traits are a good reason to Screen In a dating partner. Watch for these following traits, as they're rare to find, and enjoy this person when you find the following:

- **Love**—a feeling of deep affection.
- **Joy**—a feeling of immense pleasure and happiness.
- **Peace**—freedom from inner disturbance; tranquility.
- **Patience**—accepting delay or trouble without getting angry or upset.
- **Kindness**—being friendly, generous, and considerate.
- **Goodness**—being morally good; virtuous.
- **Faithfulness**—being faithful; staying loyal and steadfast.
- **Gentleness**—softness of action; being kind, tender, or mild-mannered.
- **Self-control**—controlling one's emotions especially in demanding situations.

Of course, these traits can be used to Screen Out as well, by finding the opposite of each trait. See examples below:

- Love's Opposite: *Hate*—intense or passionate dislike.
- Joy's Opposite: *Misery*—showing great unhappiness.
- Peace's Opposite: *Disruption*—disturbance which interrupts internally.
- Patience's Opposite: *Irritability*—bad tempered, impatient.
- Kindness's Opposite: *Meanness*—spitefulness, unfairness.

- Goodness's Opposite: **Unscrupulousness**—extremely unpleasant; dishonest.
- Faithfulness's Opposite: **Disloyalty**—absence of loyalty, devotion, or support.
- Gentleness's Opposite: **Harshness**—unpleasantly rough, cruel, or severe.
- Self-Control's Opposite: **Impropriety**—improper language, behavior, character.

These traits should send up every red flag you have in your gut. If you see any of these traits as a pattern, know there will be problems in the dating relationship surrounding that trait. Move on. NEXT. Don't hang around! Use your Dating Intelligence. Allow your gut to guide you.

Screening Tools— At a Glance

Write down this vision and clearly inscribe it."
(Habakkuk 2:2)

Bathe these Screening Tools in prayer. God will bring to your memory the ones you need in the moment.

- Pray!
- Remember: safety first.
- Project self-respect.
- Connect like a tortoise: *cautiously, wisely, slowly*.
- Know the things I value in my life and assert them.
- Know my purpose in dating.
- Know who I am at my core.
- Know what I believe about myself.
- Know what things I *refuse* to live *without*.

- Know what things I *refuse* to live *with*.
- Know what things I find *negotiable*.
- Know what things I find *non-negotiable*.
- Integrity—be true to myself.
- Objectivity—use detachment.
- Common sense—use sound judgment.
- Sanity—keep my wits about me.
- Become what I want to attract.
- Use patience—restraint.
- Exercise perseverance—resolve.
- Present polish—refinement.
- Reflect poise—composure.
- Ladies, give him the gift of the chase!
- Men, pursue!
- Go through the four seasons before engagement or marriage.
- Keep sex on the back burner.
- Sex doesn't get a man. Sex doesn't keep a man.
- Be objective: do field research.
- Learn to say to yourself: NEXT.
- Trust your gut instinct!
- Act on your gut instinct!

Screening Tools—At a Glance

- **SCREEN OUT when your date shows negative patterns from the following:**
  - Family forces—extreme opposites.
  - Communication style and flow— blocked discussions.
  - Independence versus dependence—possible codependency and control.
  - Fire and ice—hot or cold, rather than warm and cool.
  - Energy balance or imbalance—no mutual easy flow.
  - Spacing and pacing—cannot be negotiated.
  - Red flags—trust your gut; say NEXT; move on.
  - Misalignment of interests—boring and frustrating.
  - Emotional age—screen out the immature and juvenile.
  - Mental disorders—confirmed through the DSM-5.

- **SCREEN IN if your date shows a pattern of showing the following:**
  - Love
  - Joy
  - Peace
  - Patience
  - Kindness

- Goodness
- Faithfulness
- Gentleness
- Self-control

Screen OUT if your date shows a pattern of showing the following:

- Hate
- Misery
- Disruption
- Irritability
- Meanness
- Unscrupulousness
- Disloyalty
- Harshness
- Impropriety

The Ideal

These Screening Tools listed above are the ideal—the real will be some mix of the above. They are tools to help you to observe with your eyes and hear with your ears, and intuit by your gut, if the person you are dating is good for you for the long-term.

Screening Tools—At a Glance

Study these Screening Tools, "showing yourself approved" (2 Timothy 2:15), and you'll find they come back to you when you are on a date as you observe and intuit by your gut who is right or wrong for you. You're developing Dating Intelligence.

Don't be afraid! Put your values out in front of you acting as a shield to ward off sexual predators, who want sex from you—and nothing more.

Speak of your values often and with honesty: your values will both attract the person right for you and ward off the person wrong for you. Remember to do no harm as you screen.

You know God's plan for you is for good and not for evil. You can now—with your Screening Tools and Dating Intelligence—go out shrewd as a snake and harmless as a dove to begin your field research in attracting that partner that GOD has just for you. The only controls you have on a date are your own shrewd skills and screening tools. Remember that your date must make his or her own decisions, but you have a much better chance of seeing this person clearly once you have "studied to show yourself approved." (2 Timothy 2:15) Then you'll know whether to say NEXT and move on—or move forward to a second or third or fourth date. May His guiding hand be with you as you trust your brain and your gut to steer you down the right path for you.

MEET THE AUTHOR

Born and raised in Oklahoma, now a Texan, Dianna Sells, Ph.D., Author, Educator, Speaker, Professional Christian Counselor, and Coach carries her degrees from University of Oklahoma, with her B.A. in English and Speech; Oral Roberts University, with her M.A. in Christian Counseling Psychology; and LaSalle University, with her Ph.D. in Christian Counseling Psychology. Over the life of her career, she has been a professional content writer and copy editor for an international Christian publishing house in Tulsa, Oklahoma, in addition to seven years acting as a first-level Recruiter and Educator in the M.B.T.I. for the same publisher. In addition, she taught primarily High School Seniors for 10 years, mostly at Victory Christian School, Tulsa, Oklahoma, with her focus on teaching how to write with style and college prep. Her expertise in the counseling field has evolved into more than thirty years of helping Married Couples, Christian Singles, and Divorced and Widowed Christian Singles, to discover the ways to find Healthy Love in a world of deception, dilemmas, and lies. Dr. Sells has been called by God to "author a book one day" since she was 19 years old.